POLAR
HABITATS

Written by
Alex Hall

American adaptation copyright © 2026 by North Star Editions, Mendota Heights, MN 55120. All rights reserved. No part of this book may be reproduced or utilized in any form or by any means without written permission from the publisher.

Polar © 2024 BookLife Publishing
This edition is published by arrangement with BookLife Publishing

sales@northstareditions.com
888-417-0195

Library of Congress Control Number:
2024953018

ISBN
979-8-89359-320-4 (library bound)
979-8-89359-404-1 (paperback)
979-8-89359-377-8 (epub)
979-8-89359-350-1 (hosted ebook)

All facts, statistics, web addresses and URLs in this book were verified as valid and accurate at time of writing. No responsibility for any changes to external websites or references can be accepted by either the author or publisher.

Printed in the United States of America
Mankato, MN
092025

Written by:
Alex Hall

Edited by:
Noah Leatherland

Designed by:
Jasmine Pointer

Image Credits

All images are courtesy of Shutterstock.com. With thanks to Getty Images, Thinkstock Photo and iStockphoto.

Cover – Remo_Designer, The img, PavKon. Throughout – Remo_Designer, The img, SunshineVector. 4–5 – Barks, Willyam Bradberry, Ward Poppe, Petr Salinger, IndianSummer, ace03. 6–7 – Andrei Stepanov, nwdph, baldezh, Moleng24. 8–9 – Alexey Seafarer, Andrei Stepanov, Vladimir Melnikov. 10–11 – Rumka vodki, Mateusz Boinski, Ken Griffiths. 12–13 – Risto Raunio, vladsilver, TETSU Snowdrop. 14–15 – Dolores M. Harvey, Vladimir Melnik. 16–17 – Ondrej Prosicky, Mircea Costina. 18–19 – evaurban, AnnstasAg. 20–21 – Stuedal, Norenko Andrey, Leonid Sorokin. 22–23 – Vladimir Protasov2323, Alexey Seafarer.

CONTENTS

Page 4	Habitats Around the World
Page 6	Polar Climate
Page 8	Wildlife
Page 10	Polar Plants
Page 12	Emperor Penguins
Page 14	Harp Seals
Page 16	Polar Bears
Page 18	Life Cycles
Page 20	Protect the Poles
Page 22	Our Polar Journey
Page 24	Glossary and Index

Words that look like <u>this</u> can be found in the glossary on page 24.

HABITATS AROUND THE WORLD

I'm an animal expert who explores habitats around the world. A habitat is the home where animals, plants, and other living things live. Would you like to explore some amazing habitats with me?

Polar habitats are located near Earth's north and south <u>poles</u>. The North Pole is in the Arctic. The South Pole is in Antarctica. Let's explore the habitats at both poles!

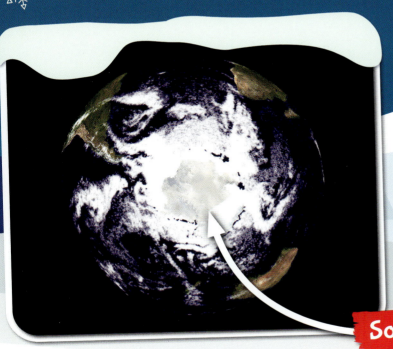

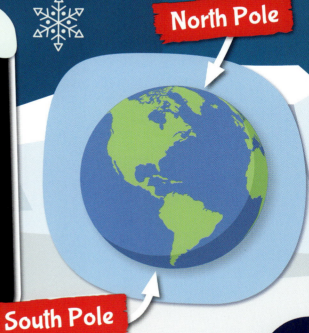

North Pole

South Pole

POLAR CLIMATE

Climate is the usual weather that happens in a place. Polar climates don't get much direct sunlight. The sun is lower in the sky at the poles. This means the ground stays cold and icy.

WILDLIFE

Thousands of animals live in polar habitats. They have <u>adapted</u> to survive in the cold.

Arctic foxes wrap their tails around themselves. This keeps them warm while they sleep.

Arctic hares have white coats in the winter. They <u>camouflage</u> themselves in the ice and snow.

It is hard to find food in the Arctic in the winter. Reindeer have adapted to need less food during this time of year.

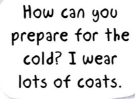

How can you prepare for the cold? I wear lots of coats.

POLAR PLANTS

Reindeer live in the Arctic tundra. They eat a plant called lichen. They eat so much lichen that it is often called reindeer moss.

Lichen

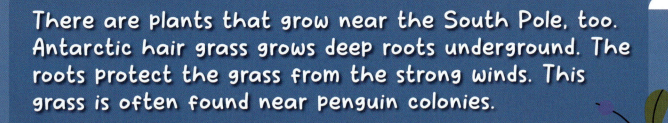

There are plants that grow near the South Pole, too. Antarctic hair grass grows deep roots underground. The roots protect the grass from the strong winds. This grass is often found near penguin colonies.

Speaking of penguins, let's go look for some.

Antarctic hair grass

EMPEROR PENGUINS

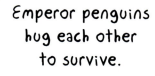

Emperor penguins live in Antarctica. They are the largest type of penguin on Earth. They huddle together to stay warm. They also huddle to protect each other from the cold winds.

Emperor penguins hug each other to survive.

Emperor penguins are excellent divers. Their wings act like big flippers. They dive underwater to find and catch fish. They can hold their breath underwater for nearly 30 minutes.

HARP SEALS

We are back in the Arctic with some harp seals. Harp seals are <u>mammals</u>. They spend most of their lives swimming in the Arctic. They eat almost anything they can find underwater.

Harp seals are carnivores, which means they only eat meat.

Baby harp seals are born with fur to keep them warm. They shed their fur as they get older. Then they grow a thick layer of fat called blubber. Blubber helps to keep them warm on the ice and in the water.

POLAR BEARS

Polar bears are the Arctic's top <u>predator</u>. Polar bears mostly eat seals. They hunt for seals by waiting near holes in the ice. They try to catch any seals that come up for air.

Male polar bears can weigh up to 1,800 pounds (800 kg).

Polar bears can swim long distances. Their huge paws help them paddle through the water. They have thick fur and blubber to keep them warm.

Let's learn more about the life of this bear.

LIFE CYCLES

Life cycles are the different stages a living thing goes through. Polar bears are mammals. They give birth to young to continue their life cycle. Baby polar bears are called cubs.

Polar bear cubs drink their mother's milk until they are old enough to hunt on their own. At around eight months old, polar bear cubs learn to hunt for food by watching their mother.

They are cute and ferocious!

PROTECT THE POLES

Polar bears spend most of their lives on the ice. However, ice is starting to melt more quickly because of <u>climate change</u>. The melting ice makes life much harder for many Arctic animals.

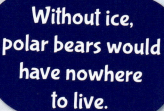

Without ice, polar bears would have nowhere to live.

However, you can help! Climate change is caused by <u>fossil fuels</u> from cars and factories. Try walking, biking, or taking the bus to school instead of driving. These steps can all help slow down climate change.

OUR POLAR JOURNEY

Brrrr! Polar habitats are very cold. But they are also very cool! We have learned so many interesting things about polar habitats and the living things in them.

GLOSSARY

adapted	changed over time to improve the chances of survival
camouflage	blending into the surroundings to hide
climate change	a crisis involving changes in the typical weather or temperature of a place
fossil fuels	fuels such as coal, oil, and gas, which formed millions of years ago from the remains of animals and plants
mammals	animals that are warm blooded, have a backbone, and produce milk to feed their children
poles	the most northern and southern parts of Earth
predator	an animal that hunts other animals for food

INDEX

Antarctica 5, 7, 11–12
Arctic, the 5, 9, 10, 14, 16, 20
fish 13
fur 15, 17
ice 9, 15–16, 20
plants 4, 10–11
snow 7, 9
winds 7, 11–12